Write with the Lord

40 QUICK QUIET TIMES FOR AUTHORS

J.D. REMPEL

SILVER DOOR
PUBLISHING

Cover Design by Hannah Linder Designs

Edited by Julie Harbison

WRITE WITH THE LORD: 40 QUICK QUIET TIMES FOR AUTHORS

Copyright © 2025 by J.D. Rempel
Published by Silver Door Publishing, LLC.
Dublin, California 94568
www.silverdoorpublishing.com

ISBN 979-8-9929291-0-2 (Paperback)
ISBN 979-8-9929291-1-9 (Ebook)
ISBN 979-8-9929291-2-6 (Audiobook)
Library of Congress Control Number: 2025910577

Published in the United States of America

INTRODUCTION

As Christian writers we have received a special gift from the Lord: a calling to write. Our audiences may be different, as some write to Christians, to the secular market, or to both. With the Holy Spirit living inside us, we can boldly proclaim and spread the Truth of His Word through our writing. This is why we need to be diligent in our prayers and commit time each day to dedicate our work to Him and allow Him to work through us. God is our partner in writing, and we should be asking Him for guidance, protection, and fruit from our labor. So each day, let's begin our writing by focusing on Him and His will for our ministry.

AUTHOR'S NOTE

Since writing is largely a solitary endeavor, I've used plural pronouns to create a sense of togetherness for most of the devotional parts. But there are times where I felt led to change point of view and share some of my personal encounters or directly encourage you.

FOREWORD

We writers are slightly left of plumb, yes? We spend hours by ourselves creating stories that didn't exist before our fingers hit the keyboard or delve deep into an area of life that can teach others lessons that will carry them for years.

Yet we know we can't live a solitary life. We need friends, we need family, and we need each other—other writers who understand the somewhat neurotic world we live in.

And we need encouragement, oh how we need encouragement. After coaching, speaking to, and working with writers for more than fifteen years, I've found the greatest need writers have is to be encouraged. It's why I'm so glad you're holding this book in your hands. Because it will light up your mind, light up your heart, light up your spirit and soul, and I'm guessing you need that.

Maybe it's just me and my writer friends, but I'm guessing it's you as well, the tendency to neglect our hearts; our tendency to get "just a few more pages written!" rather than tend to the gardening of our greatest treasure. Proverbs tells us to guard our hearts above all else. Let's read that phrase again. Guard our hearts above all else. The greatest priority of our lives should be guarding our hearts. And there's much to guard against these days. The onslaught seems ever stronger, ever louder, and ever more destructive.

So I have an idea. When you get up tomorrow morning, get your coffee (or beverage of choice) go outside and look up at the stars (if you're an early riser like me) and give thanks you've been given the gift of writing.

Come back in and ignore your phone, your computer, your email. Pick up this book and spend time watering the garden of your heart. Read Jennifer's devotion of the day. Then put the book down and meditate on what has stirred inside you.

Science tells us it takes 2 – 3 seconds to imbed a negative thought. A positive thought? Thirty seconds. No wonder Paul (in Philippians) tells us to meditate on whatever is good, whatever is pure, whatever is true. So take time to imbed the ideas the Spirit awakens in you during your time with *Write With the Lord*.

I've known Jennifer for many years now, and I can tell you she is one who has a deep love for God's children. Her desire to see this devotional reach into the deep places of your heart is palpable.

I hope her desire comes true. I hope you are refreshed and rejuvenated with every sentence you read. And I hope these pages inspire you to create pages that will inspire others beyond what they imagined.

James L. Rubart, October 2024

DIG DEEPER

I intended for these quiet times to be a swift yet uplifting part of your writing routine especially for those with a busy schedule. But if you'd like to dig deeper, I've provided a reflection section for each day.

Here are some questions to consider as you seek to fulfill God's will with your writing:

Who does God say that I am?
What is God teaching me through this writing journey?
Am I writing in obedience to God?
What can I accomplish for His Kingdom through my writing?
How can I partner with God on this project or task?

At jdrempel.com, you can download a free printable bookmark of these questions to use as you work through the devotional.

My hope is for you to be encouraged in your walk with the Lord through these daily prompts and be inspired to Write with the Lord.

DAY 1

DESIGNED FOR A PURPOSE

"For we are God's handiwork, created in Christ Jesus to do good works, which God prepared in advance for us to do."
—Ephesians 2:10

In the beginning . . .God created us to be writers. It was His plan for us all along. The writing we love and enjoy are the good works we have the honor to do for Him. We must not forget that we were meant for this purpose. It is our destiny.

Thank you, God for creating me to be a writer. And thank you for designing me to do good works for Your kingdom. When I am discouraged help me to remember that You have made me for this specific purpose. Help me to walk in this destiny that You have planned for me. In Jesus' name. Amen.

Reflection:

....

....

....

....

....

....

....

....

....

....

....

DAY 2

OUR ABILITIES

"Then Moses summoned Bezalel and Oholiab and every skilled person to whom the LORD had given ability and who was willing to come and do the work." —Exodus 36:2

As writers, God gives us the skill and ability to accomplish the task He has for us. We already have what we need to finish our stories. He has provided the time, the words, the tools for editing, the marketing, the publisher, the readers—***everything***. But we need to do the work. So let's get to it!

Lord, thank you for the skills and ability You have given me. When the task is difficult, help me to remember that I can accomplish it because You have equipped me with everything I need. I pray that I won't be lazy or put things off. Please fill me with a spirit of work and responsibility to complete this task You've entrusted to me. In Jesus' name. Amen.

Reflection:

....

....

....

....

....

....

....

....

....

....

....

DAY 3

OUR GIFT

"Each of you should use whatever gift you have received to serve others, as faithful stewards of God's grace in its various forms... If anyone serves, they should do so with the strength God provides, so that in all things God may be praised through Jesus Christ. To him be the glory and the power for ever and ever. Amen." —1 Peter 4:10, 11b

Our writing is a precious gift from the Lord. When we receive this calling, we are to use it to serve others. It is a hard endeavor, but the Lord will provide us with the strength we need to complete the work. In relying on Him, we will bring Him glory. In doing the tasks He has set before us, we will bring Him praise.

God, thank you for this glorious gift. Please help me to use it to serve others as You have called me. Remind me that You are the one who gives me strength and not to rely on myself. May I give You praise, glory, and honor in whatever I do. Let Your name be lifted high. Amen.

Reflection:

....

....

....

....

....

....

....

....

....

....

....

DAY 4

COMMIT

"Commit to the LORD whatever you do, and he will establish your plans." —Proverbs 16:3

Using this devotional is a small way in which we commit our writing to the Lord. Let's commit to taking time each day to put Him first before we put pen to paper or type one letter. But we shouldn't stop there—every step of our writing should be led by Him including the business aspects of our ministry too.

My writing is for You, Lord. May the words I craft be from You and bring glory only to You. I commit and dedicate this time for the work which You've called me. Remind me to always put You first in whatever I do and in every part of this ministry. Thank you for giving me the opportunity to serve You and the fulfillment of Your promises. In Jesus' name. Amen.

Reflection:

....

....

....

....

....

....

....

....

....

....

....

DAY 5

DEDICATING OUR WORK

"May the favor of the Lord our God rest on us; establish the work of our hands for us—yes, establish the work of our hands."
—Psalm 90:17

Everything we have comes from God—this includes our work. When we dedicate our writing to Him and ask His blessing, He will guide us and grant us a successful outcome, even if it is not one we see or measure by our own standards of success. As we fulfill the calling He has placed on our hearts, the words He gives us will not return void (Isaiah 55:11).

Lord, may Your favor rest upon me as I labor in the work You have given me. Thank you for these words that flow from my heart and into these hands. As You have promised, do not allow these words to return void. Establish the work of my hands, yes, please establish the work of my hands. In Your mighty name. Amen.

Reflection:

....

....

....

....

....

....

....

....

....

....

....

DAY 6

OUR RELATIONSHIP WITH THE LORD

"I am the vine; you are the branches. If you remain in me and I in you, you will bear much fruit; apart from me you can do nothing." —John 15:5

To grow as Christian writers we need to be fed and watered by the Lord, through prayer, by reading His Word, and through fellowship with other believers. When we spend time and depend on Him we will flourish and bear lasting fruit. We cannot do anything worthwhile on our own.

Lord, please help me to be diligent and faithful in my relationship with You. I want to know You more and to hunger and thirst for Your Word. Thank you for sustaining me and providing the Living Water that I may grow. Please use my words to bring You glory and my readers into Your Kingdom. In Jesus' name. Amen.

Reflection:

....

....

....

....

....

....

....

....

....

....

....

DAY 7

FILLED WITH THE HOLY SPIRIT

"After they prayed, the place where they were meeting was shaken. And they were all filled with the Holy Spirit and spoke the word of God boldly." —Acts 4:31

Without the Lord's help, we cannot speak His message boldly to others. We need to pray that the Holy Spirit will empower and guide us. He will instruct us with words so that our readers will be able to understand who He is.

Lord, I want to speak your words confidently. Fill me with the Holy Spirit's power to proclaim the message You've given me. Thank you for this opportunity to serve You through my calling. In the power of the Holy Spirit. Amen.

Reflection:

....

....

....

....

....

....

....

....

....

....

....

DAY 8

A WITNESS

"But you will receive power when the Holy Spirit comes on you; and you will be my witnesses in Jerusalem, and in all Judea and Samaria, and to the ends of the earth." —Acts 1:8

Sometimes when I'm writing, I feel the Holy Spirit come upon me. It's like I can hear the Lord saying, "Yes, this is exactly what I want you to write." It's that assurance which keeps me going and inspires me. I acknowledge these moments to remind myself I am doing the Lord's will and I am being His witness to my readers.

Lord, please work through me to make your message known to my readers and to those in the world. Help me to listen to Your voice. If there is something You do not want me to write, stop me and show me the right words. I want to do Your will and share Your Truth. Thank you for affirming my calling. Please use me to minister to others. In Jesus' name. Amen.

Reflection:

....

....

....

....

....

....

....

....

....

....

....

DAY 9

OUR MARKET

"Nevertheless, each person should live as a believer in whatever situation the Lord has assigned to them, just as God has called them." —1 Corinthians 7:17a

Writing is our calling from the Lord. Each of us has an assigned task the Lord has given to us. Our markets and audience may be different but our lives are to be a living example to all.

Lord, thank you for the calling you have put on my life. Please, help me to use it for Your glory. May the words I write and speak bring others into a deeper understanding of who You are. For the unbelievers, I pray that the light of You in my life will shine brightly so they will be drawn into a relationship with You. For my brothers and sisters in Christ, I pray for a closer relationship with You as they learn more about who You are. And Lord, I pray that I will draw closer to You and only use the words You have given me and not my own. In Jesus' name. Amen.

Reflection:

....

....

....

....

....

....

....

....

....

....

....

DAY 10

OUR RETURN

"As the rain and the snow come down from heaven, and do not return to it without watering the earth and making it bud and flourish, so that it yields seed for the sower and bread for the eater, so is my word that goes out from my mouth: It will not return to me empty, but will accomplish what I desire and achieve the purpose for which I sent it."—Isaiah 55:10-11

Sometimes our writing doesn't reach the large audience we had hoped. It's so much easier when we have success, but success is never guaranteed in this world. But what if our writing changed or touched just one person? Then, our obedience will have done something great for the kingdom of God, and He will be pleased with us.

Lord, help me to remember You don't measure success the way the world does. When I am disappointed in the results, grant me a spirit of perseverance to continue the work for which you have called me. Thank you that the words You have given me will not return empty. Please use my writing to impact Your kingdom for Your glory. Let the words I write achieve the purpose for which You have for them. In Jesus' name. Amen.

Reflection:

....

....

....

....

....

....

....

....

....

....

....

DAY 11

FAITHFULNESS

"His master replied, 'Well done, good and faithful servant! You have been faithful with a few things; I will put you in charge of many things. Come and share your master's happiness!'"
—Matthew 25:21

Faithfulness in our work is what the Lord requires from us. It is so important that Jesus used the word "faithful" twice. He wants us to keep moving forward and strive to finish our tasks. And if we use our talents, we will produce a gain. In the parable, the only servant who failed was the one who didn't do anything.

Lord, thank you for this work and the talents You have given me. Please help me to remain faithful to the tasks You have laid out for me. Let my gain bring honor and glory to You. In Your name. Amen.

Reflection:

....

....

....

....

....

....

....

....

....

....

....

DAY 12

PRAY FOR A HARVEST

"And he directed the people to sit down on the grass. Taking the five loaves and the two fish and looking up to heaven, he gave thanks and broke the loaves. Then he gave them to the disciples, and the disciples gave them to the people. They all ate and were satisfied, and the disciples picked up twelve basketfuls of broken pieces that were left over."—Matthew 14:19-20

As with the miracle of the five thousand, God can turn our five loaves of bread and two fish, our writing, into something which can "feed" the multitudes. When our readers consume our words, we want them to be satisfied. Believe that God will do this and thank Him for the harvest to come.

Lord, I believe that You will use the words You have given me to bless others and glorify Your name. Thank you for the harvest You will provide. Allow my words to satisfy and fulfill my readers and draw them into a relationship with You. In Your name. Amen.

Reflection:

....

....

....

....

....

....

....

....

....

....

....

DAY 13

CLEAR DIRECTION

"Whether you turn to the right or to the left, your ears will hear a voice behind you, saying, 'This is the way; walk in it.'"
—Isaiah 30:21

As writers, we have so many decisions to make about our careers. What idea, article, or book should we work on? What should we do about marketing? Should we find an agent? Do we traditionally publish or self-publish? Is this the right place to submit? Our choices are endless. But we are blessed to have Someone who walks beside us and guides us along the way.

Lord, please give me ears to hear where You want me to go and what You want me to do. Help me to listen to the Holy Spirit. When I'm unsure, give me the wisdom to make the decision You have planned for me. Thank you for directing my steps. In Your precious name. Amen.

Reflection:

....

....

....

....

....

....

....

....

....

....

....

DAY 14

HANDLING THE TRUTH OF GOD'S WORD

"Do your best to present yourself to God as one approved, a worker who does not need to be ashamed and who correctly handles the word of truth." —2 Timothy 2:15

When we use Scripture or a spiritual truth, we should be careful to convey it as the Lord intended. The Word of God is living and active (Hebrews 4:12) applying to us today, but we should not taint the meaning of His Word to promote our own agendas or beliefs.

Lord, thank you for the honor of being a messenger of Your love to this world. Teach me Your Word and how to handle it correctly. Get rid of any pridefulness in my heart. Let me speak Your words only. Help me share the understanding of Your Truth in the way which will benefit my readers to draw closer to You. In Jesus' name. Amen.

Reflection:

....

....

....

....

....

....

....

....

....

....

....

DAY 15

OUR LIGHT

"You are the light of the world. A town built on a hill cannot be hidden. Neither do people light a lamp and put it under a bowl. Instead they put it on its stand, and it gives light to everyone in the house. In the same way, let your light shine before others, that they may see your good deeds and glorify your Father in heaven." —Matthew 5:14-16

Writing is a part of our witness to others of God's love and faithfulness. The deeper we know the Lord, the brighter our light will shine. People will see Him in us and in the things we write. Our stories will become a beacon of the hope we have in Him.

Lord, thank you for being my Light and my salvation and for pulling me out of darkness. Help me to shine Your Light to the world, personally and professionally. Please use me to draw my readers into a relationship with You. Let my light shine before others so they may see Your good works and glorify You. In Your name. Amen.

Reflection:

....

....

....

....

....

....

....

....

....

....

....

DAY 16

OUR PROTECTION

"My prayer is not that you take them out of the world but that you protect them from the evil one." —John 17:15

My most spiritual project was the hardest one to write. I didn't think that my project was significant enough for Satan to thwart, but I was wrong. As I strived to write and type my manuscript, the Holy Spirit flooded over me with the indescribable beauty of His presence. The act of writing became and continues to be an incredible blessing which has drawn me closer to the Lord.

Thank you, Lord for protecting me from the evil one. And thank you for giving me the Holy Spirit to guide and help me. In everything I do, please remind me that You are with me and that I am never alone. Give me the strength to finish the work You have called me to do. In Your Precious name. Amen.

Reflection:

....

....

....

....

....

....

....

....

....

....

....

DAY 17

FEELING OVERWHELMED

"Cast all your anxiety on him because he cares for you."
—1 Peter 5:7

Our "to-do" list seems endless. We work but see little progress. Stop, drop, and pray! Give these burdens to the Lord and seek His will for what needs to be done. He will answer!

Lord, some days my burdens are so hard to bear. I'm overwhelmed and need Your help. Guide me in the tasks You want me to do, and if I'm taking on too much show me what You want me to let go. Thank you for walking by my side and shouldering the load with me. In Jesus' name. Amen.

Reflection:

....

....

....

....

....

....

....

....

....

....

....

DAY 18

WAITING OR PROCRASTINATION

"Be very careful, then, how you live—not as unwise but as wise, making the most of every opportunity, because the days are evil. Therefore do not be foolish, but understand what the Lord's will is." —Ephesians 5:15-17

When our writing seems to be at a standstill, we need to figure out why. Is the Lord stopping us? Is it Satan working against us? Or is it our own sinful self? If it is the latter two, then it's procrastination, and we need to fight through it with prayer. If it is the Lord putting our project on hold, it's the same solution. Use prayer to determine His will as you wait on the Lord.

Lord, I need wisdom from You. If I am procrastinating, please help me to push through it. If You want me to wait, please give me understanding so I may do what is right. I seek to do Your will. Thank you for this opportunity to serve You. In Your Son's name. Amen.

Reflection:

....

....

....

....

....

....

....

....

....

....

....

DAY 19

DISTRACTIONS

"But Jesus often withdrew to lonely places and prayed."
—Luke 5:16

Sometimes there are personal things in our lives that can distract us from our writing: a problem we can't solve, responsibilities that clamor for our time and attention, and things which are out of our control. Find a place where you can get away to pray and receive comfort and encouragement from our Savior, even if only for a moment. Use those times as an opportunity to cling to our God and seek Him.

Lord, I have no control over my life, but You do. I know that I can lay my burdens down at Your feet. But when I need to carry them, You will help me shoulder the load. Lord, I desire Your peace in these circumstances. Remind me I can cling to You because You are my fortress and deliverer and my help in trouble. Thank you for giving me the Holy Spirit so that I am never alone. In Jesus' name. Amen.

Reflection:

....

....

....

....

....

....

....

....

....

....

DAY 20

A FALLOW SEASON

"There is a time for everything, and a season for every activity under the heavens... He has made everything beautiful in its time." —Ecclesiastes 3:1, 11a

Sometimes life gets in the way of our plans to write. And we don't know when we'll be able to write again. Do not be disappointed or discouraged. God sees and knows. His plans for you will succeed at just the right time. He can use this minute, hour, day, week, month, or year to give you rest, develop your character, or reveal things to you. He always has a purpose.

God, even if I can't write today, please use me to bring glory to Your name. Please open my eyes, ears, and heart for what you are teaching me at this time in my life. Thank you for this time that I can cling to You and know that I'm good enough just as Your child. In Jesus' name. Amen.

Reflection:

....

....

....

....

....

....

....

....

....

....

....

DAY 21

OPEN DOOR

"I know your deeds. See, I have placed before you an open door that no one can shut. I know that you have little strength, yet you have kept my word and have not denied my name."
—Revelation 3:8

When God has called us to a task, the way will be open. This doesn't mean there won't be obstacles, but no one can shut the door God has opened for us—including ourselves. The end goal of God's purposes will be fulfilled. Even in our weaknesses and our struggles, there is a path before us no one can take away. Remain faithful to Him and walk through that open door.

Lord, I'm facing challenges on every side. Show me the way to the open door You have provided for me. Help me to avoid and ignore the distractions. Thank you for Your Word which is a lamp to my feet and a light to my path. You are where my help comes from. I want to be faithful to the calling You have given me. In Jesus' name. Amen.

Reflection:

....

....

....

....

....

....

....

....

....

....

....

DAY 22

SPEAKING

"My heart is stirred by a noble theme as I recite my verses for the king; my tongue is the pen of a skillful writer."—Psalm 45:1

Some of us do not consider ourselves competent speakers. Even after practicing, oftentimes we find ourselves tongue-tied or stumble over our words. But we must keep trying because we need to be ready to share the beautiful revelations the Lord has given to our audience.

Lord, thank you for stirring my heart with this story theme. You are the One who controls my tongue. Even when I stumble over my words, please use me to glorify You. I ask that You give me the right words to share with my audience and that I will listen to the Holy Spirit. In Your name. Amen.

Reflection:

....

....

....

....

....

....

....

....

....

....

....

DAY 23

CHALLENGES

"Do not be anxious about anything, but in every situation, by prayer and petition, with thanksgiving, present your requests to God." —Philippians 4:6

A deadline is looming. An unfavorable review came out on your book. There was a negative comment about your article. Your marketing strategy flopped. In these circumstances, give thanks to God and turn your discouragement into praise. Thank the Lord that you have a deadline to meet. Seek guidance from Him as you analyze criticism for improvement. Praise Him for the knowledge you learned from marketing and what you can do better next time.

I praise You and thank You, Lord for the work You have given me. Please help me not to worry about anything and to lean on You for reassurance. Your Word says that I can cast all my cares on You and that You will sustain me. Enable me to live that truth especially in the challenges I am facing. In Your name. Amen.

Reflection:

....

....

....

....

....

....

....

....

....

....

....

DAY 24

COMBATING SELF-DOUBT

"Have I not commanded you? Be strong and courageous. Do not be afraid; do not be discouraged, for the LORD your God will be with you wherever you go." —Joshua 1:9

If God has called us to write, He will be with us. Cast aside self-doubt. God told Joshua as the leader of Israel to be strong and courageous three times, and the people also reminded him (Joshua 1). Even though our writing journey will not be easy, we do not need to fear or be discouraged—God is with us.

Thank you, Lord, for Your Presence in my life and in my heart. Remind me of Your promises. When fear and discouragement assail me, help me to remember Your Truth. I want to embrace and fulfill the calling You have on my life. In Your name. Amen.

Reflection:

....

....

....

....

....

....

....

....

....

....

....

DAY 25

COMPARISON

"You shall not covet your neighbor's house. You shall not covet your neighbor's wife, or his male or female servant, his ox or donkey, or anything that belongs to your neighbor."
—Exodus 20:17

As writers, comparison is hard to avoid since in our line of work success is measured by sales, awards, and popularity. But those are not the scales God uses. Our Loving, Heavenly Father looks at us individually. When we're feeling low or filled with self-doubt, we need to look up to Him and not around us. He's the only Judge who counts.

Thank you, Lord for this gift You have given me. Help me to keep my focus on You and not compare myself to others. When others excel, give me a sincere joy for them. And if accolades come my way, please give me a spirit of humility and thankfulness. For Your glory. Amen.

Reflection:

....

....

....

....

....

....

....

....

....

....

....

DAY 26

MY PLACE

"But in fact God has placed the parts in the body, every one of them, just as he wanted them to be." —1 Corinthians 12:18

Whether we are fiction or non-fiction writers or a mix of both, God has placed us exactly where He wants us to be. We all have the same gift, but we use it in different ways in a plethora of genres. We are unique and so are our audiences. He created our specific talent to reach and meet the needs of our intended readers.

Lord, please mold me into the writer You want me to be. Thank you for making me who I am and shaping me into a unique writer. Help me to embrace and enhance my originality to reach those You have in mind for the revelation of Your Truth. In Jesus' name. Amen.

Reflection:

....

....

....

....

....

....

....

....

....

....

....

DAY 27

UNIQUE WRITER

"I praise you because I am fearfully and wonderfully made; your works are wonderful, I know that full well."—Psalm 139:14

You are specifically designed by the Maker of the universe. The way you craft your stories, your writing style, and your voice are all part of what makes you unique. No one anytime or anywhere will ever write like you. You are one of a kind. Give thanks and praise to Him for your individuality and marvelous distinction.

Thank you, Lord, that I am fearfully and wonderfully made. The world needs me to share what You have given to me. God, help me to be everything You intended me to be. In Jesus' name. Amen.

Reflection:

....

....

....

....

....

....

....

....

....

....

....

DAY 28

TRUTH BEHIND THE FICTION

"A good man brings good things out of the good stored up in his heart, and an evil man brings evil things out of the evil stored up in his heart. For the mouth speaks what the heart is full of."
—Luke 6:45

As fiction writers, our minds live in a place of make believe. We can spend days, weeks, months, or even years in these worlds which we create. But the ultimate story is the Truth of the redemptive work of Jesus Christ. As believers, this is the story that dwells in our hearts and is evident in our lives. The love of the Lord should be behind every word we write so our readers will know the Truth behind the fiction.

Lord, help me to create a fictional world that reflects You and Your goodness and mercy. Let my characters speak the Truth of Your Word. Thank you for Your sacrifice. Please use my writing to reach others for You. In Jesus' name. Amen.

Reflection:

....

....

....

....

....

....

....

....

....

....

....

DAY 29

INSPIRATION

"As the deer pants for streams of water, so my soul pants for you, my God." —Psalm 42:1

The Scriptures are filled with the beauty of Who God is and what He has done for us. Its magnificent imagery and Jesus' own life and words capture the majesty of our Lord and His marvelous works. He is our ultimate source of inspiration.

Lord, let my words be filled with the beauty of You. Thank you for the inspiration and creativity abounding around and inside me. Use me as an instrument to declare the wonders of You to the world. In Jesus' name. Amen.

Reflection:

....

....

....

....

....

....

....

....

....

....

....

DAY 30

WRITING COMMUNITY

"And let us consider how we may spur one another on toward love and good deeds, not giving up meeting together, as some are in the habit of doing, but encouraging one another—and all the more as you see the Day approaching." —Hebrews 10:24-25

Writing can be a lonely endeavor. We need community. Find a group where you feel accepted and encouraged with people who build you up but also challenge and invigorate you. If that place ceases to be right for you, move on, but keep searching until you discover your tribe or build one of your own.

Thank you, Lord that You have provided a place for me. Please, lead me to a group which will help me grow into the person and writer You want me to be. Also, help me to contribute and build up others in the community. In Jesus' name. Amen.

Reflection:

....

....

....

....

....

....

....

....

....

....

....

DAY 31

CALLED FOR A PURPOSE

"And we know that in all things God works for the good of those who love him, who have been called according to his purpose." —Romans 8:28

Our writing can seem like a long, hard road, but we've been called to this purpose. If we persevere through hardship and doubt, God will make something good and beautiful from our efforts. And when we walk in obedience to Him, He will use us to bring about His ultimate, everlasting goal.

Thank you, Lord, that at the end of this journey, You'll have made something good from my efforts. Please help me persevere through the difficulties and use me for Your purpose. I love you, Lord. In Jesus' name. Amen.

Reflection:

....

....

....

....

....

....

....

....

....

....

....

DAY 32

LEARNING AND SKILL

"If the ax is dull and its edge unsharpened, more strength is needed but skill will bring success." —Ecclesiastes 10:10

We need to be constantly learning about all aspects of our craft. It may seem daunting, but the more we study and practice, the sharper we will become. As we progress in skills and expertise our tasks will become less difficult. And in time we can pass on this knowledge to others.

God, please hone this gift so that I may be sharp, alert, and prepared for the task that You have set before me. I want to be a tool used for Your glory. Thank you for providing opportunities to learn. Please help me to grow in knowledge and in Truth. In Your name. Amen.

Reflection:

....
....
....
....
....
....
....
....
....
....
....

DAY 33

ONE AUDIENCE

"Am I now trying to win the approval of human beings, or of God? Or am I trying to please people? If I were still trying to please people, I would not be a servant of Christ."
—Galatians 1:10

As servants of Christ, we already have our Master's approval. But our human nature seeks acceptance and acknowledgement from the world. We must remember we have One Audience and it is only Him we need to please.

Lord, thank you for accepting me for who I am. I want to be a faithful and good servant and use my gift to honor You. Please show me how I can please You today. In Jesus' name. Amen.

Reflection:

....

....

....

....

....

....

....

....

....

....

....

DAY 34

OUR UNSAVED READERS

"Pray also for me, that whenever I speak, words may be given me so that I will fearlessly make known the mystery of the gospel," —Ephesians 6:19

Our writing is a ministry. Through our books and stories God can reach the hearts of unbelievers. With our words and actions, we can show His love for them and share with them the good news of the gospel.

Lord, let the words that I write be pleasing in Your sight. Please use them to bring others into a relationship with You. I want to be a light to others so that they may come to know You. Give me boldness to share Your Word. Thank you for allowing me to be part of Your plan to draw others to You. In Your name. Amen.

Reflection:

....

....

....

....

....

....

....

....

....

....

....

DAY 35

OPPORTUNITIES

"Give careful thought to the paths for your feet and be steadfast in all your ways." —Proverbs 4:26

Before we submit to an agent or publisher, we need to make sure that is where the Lord has directed us. How do we do that? By praying about it and seeking His will through Scripture. This also applies when working with others, whether they are believers or unbelievers. Sometimes the open door isn't the one we are supposed to walk through. We need to continually seek the Lord's will for our writing.

Lord, a path has opened up before me. Is this where You are leading me or do I need to wait? Please guide me as I move forward. Thank you that You walk with me along this writing and publishing journey. I want to do Your will; please show me the way. In Your name. Amen.

Reflection:

....

....

....

....

....

....

....

....

....

....

....

DAY 36

CLEAN WORDS

"May these words of my mouth and this meditation of my heart be pleasing in your sight, LORD, my Rock and my Redeemer."
—Psalm 19:14

Sometimes, our writing requires that we illustrate evil, so that we can present the redemptive work of Christ. But we need to be thoughtful and careful with the words and images we portray. We should be guiding our readers toward Jesus and to a relationship with Him, not glorifying evil. We must check our hearts and stay in the Word to keep our hearts and minds fixed on Christ.

Lord, thank you for being my Rock and my Redeemer. Allow the words that I write to be pleasing in Your sight. Let them reflect the Truth of Your Word and be a blessing. With these words, fill my readers with joy and encouragement. Help them see You through my writing. In Your name. Amen.

Reflection:

....

....

....

....

....

....

....

....

....

....

....

DAY 37

OUR BEST

"Whatever you do, work at it with all your heart, as working for the Lord, not for human masters, ... It is the Lord Christ you are serving." —Colossians 3:23, 24b

Some parts of writing and the writing business can seem like a drudgery. Throughout the process, whether it is easy or difficult, we need to give the Lord our best effort. It can be hard, but our perseverance will produce for us fruit from our labor and bring honor and glory to our King.

God, thank you for this opportunity to serve You. Please help me to be diligent in the task You have set before me. Keep my heart and mind focused on You and what You want me to do. Let this work bring honor and glory to You. In Your name. Amen.

Reflection:

....

....

....

....

....

....

....

....

....

....

....

DAY 38

THE WRITING BUSINESS

"I am sending you out like sheep among wolves. Therefore be as shrewd as snakes and as innocent as doves."—Matthew 10:16

The snake is adaptable, and the dove is harmless. And both creatures are smart in their own ways. As writers we must be wise with our finances, time, and the people we work with. We should also be flexible and beyond reproach in our business dealings. Our profession is in part a ministry and should reflect the principles of honor and integrity as a witness to others.

God, thank you for my writing. As I serve You, help me to be wise in all aspects of this business. I want to be a good example of a Christian professional with integrity. May my finances, time, and partnerships throughout my career bring honor to You. In Your name. Amen.

Reflection:

....
....
....
....
....
....
....
....
....
....
....

DAY 39

TRUST

"Trust in the LORD with all your heart and lean not on your own understanding; in all your ways submit to him, and he will make your paths straight." —Proverbs 3:5-6

God is the Ultimate Author. He knows the whole story and our place in it. Unlike our own fictional characters, God is not surprised by what we do and the outcome. When we acknowledge Him, He will show us the way we need to go.

Thank you, Lord for Your guidance. I want to trust You more. Please forgive my doubts. You are the One Who knows the entire story. I acknowledge You, and that I need to lean on Your understanding to know Your will for my life. In Jesus' name. Amen.

Reflection:

....

....

....

....

....

....

....

....

....

....

....

DAY 40

CONFIDENCE FOR COMPLETION

"being confident of this, that he who began a good work in you will carry it on to completion until the day of Christ Jesus."
—Philippians 1:6

Sometimes our projects overwhelm us with the multitude of tasks we need to undertake to finish. But keep moving forward step by step in confidence. Every word we write or every activity we perform for publishing is an act toward completion.

Lord, thank you that You will carry out Your purpose in me. Please give me confidence when I'm feeling overwhelmed. Let me experience the joy of celebration whenever I move forward in faith, no matter how small the step. Please give me the vision of the future You want to complete in me. In Your name. Amen.

Reflection:

....

....

....

....

....

....

....

....

....

....

....

OTHER BOOKS

by J.D. Rempel

Marigold and the Snoring King (Picture Book)

The NorCal Girls series (Girls ages 8-13)

Melanie on the Move

Melanie at Camp Redwoods

Melanie versus Middle School

Find out more about J.D. and her books at jdrempel.com

www.ingramcontent.com/pod-product-compliance
Lightning Source LLC
Chambersburg PA
CBHW031225120626
46545CB00003B/1003